Exploring

getting to know your world

A Puffin Book
Written and produced by McPhee Gribble Publishers
Illustrated by Jenny Elliott

Exploring your world

You don't have to be a long way from home to go exploring.

Exploring really means finding out all there is to know about something or somewhere – by using your eyes and ears and sometimes keeping very still.

Wherever you live there are living things to get to know. Cities and towns as well as country places are full of wild life once you know where to look.

There are birds that have learnt to live with people and buildings. There are insects and small creatures lurking in safe dark corners. There are plants creeping over piles of rubble and through cracks in concrete.

People share the world with countless living things. We are only one kind of life that needs fresh air and water and sunshine and food to survive.

Every living thing needs other living things. There is an endless chain of life that should not be broken.

But we break the chain all the time – and live as if no other kinds of life matter at all.

Each time a country path is concreted over, or a watering hole dries up, or a factory pours smoke out into the air, or farm animals and pets escape and take over from wild creatures – the chain is broken, perhaps forever.

Exploring your neighbourhood is the best way to get to know for yourself how things happen.

This book is about some of the things you could look for. Once you start, you will be able to find many more.

Gear

You can make some special equipment to help you see things clearly. Animals and birds and fish can be watched without them knowing you are there.

Cut the bottom off a large plastic bottle.

Bend a piece of waxed cardboard and stitch or staple the join.

An underwater viewer can be made from a juice bottle or a piece of stiff cardboard.

For looking into nests without disturbing birds, tie a car or bike mirror to a long stick. Keep the mirror out of the sun or the bird will be frightened by the flashes.

A periscope lets you look around corners or over the top of walls or crowds. Make one from stiff cardboard and two pocket mirrors.

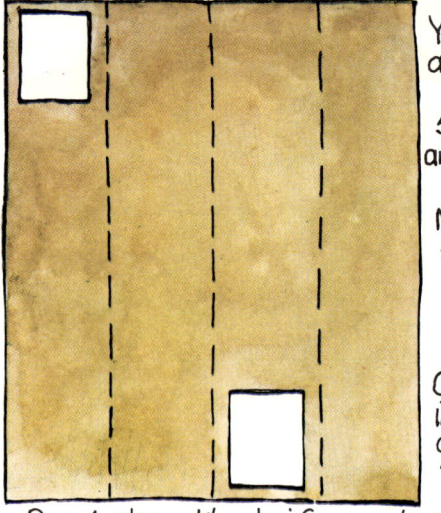

You will need a rectangle of cardboard 50 cm high and 32 cm wide.

Mark 4 even strips with the back of a knife.

Cut a hole in the first and third strips.

Bend along the knife marks and tape the box shape together.

hole

mirror

hole

mirror

Make 2 triangles from cardboard to fit inside the box.

Glue a mirror to each triangle.

Make a tree-hide for watching birds. Start at nest-building time so the birds will get used to you before their eggs are laid.

Look for signs of burrows or footprints to choose a place where animals pass.

Build the hide quietly and carefully using bushes and grass. Make it very hard to see. Leave room to lie down to watch when you have a long wait.

The best way to have a close look at an insect that might bite is with a jam jar and a piece of stiff cardboard.

Collect other useful things as well.

Beaches

On any low sea shore you can find small living creatures and sea plants. Sand dunes, salt marshes and rocky shores have their different kinds of life. Each living thing has worked out its own way to live with the sea.

Limpets and barnacles are smooth and cling to rocks so the waves can't move them. Try prising one off with your fingers and feel its strength.

Look for tiny sandhoppers, crabs with legs made for digging and sandworms with breathing tubes that stick up above the sand.

High up the beach you can find green seaweed such as sea-lettuce. It is green because it has learnt to live in the air and sunlight as land plants do.

Midway between high and low tide levels are the brown seaweeds. In deeper water near the shore the red seaweeds grow. These are hardly ever uncovered by the water.

In some places you can find a flat brown seaweed called kelp. Take a fresh damp piece home and nail it up outside.

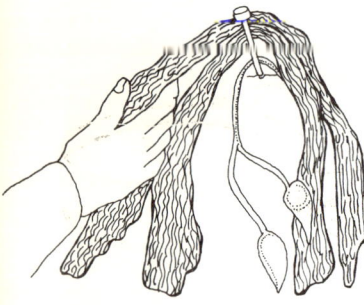

Kelp acts as a weather forecaster.

In fine dry weather the kelp is dry, too. When the air is damp the kelp looks limp and glossy.

You could make an underwater viewer to look into rock pools. Cut one out from a large juice bottle or a piece of waxed cardboard. Watch for a long time and you will start to see many happenings under water.

A shovel and a large garden sieve or kitchen strainer help you to look closely at the sand dwellers.

Choose a place near the water's edge to dig. Take a deep shovelful of sand as quickly as you can or many things will sense danger and vanish.

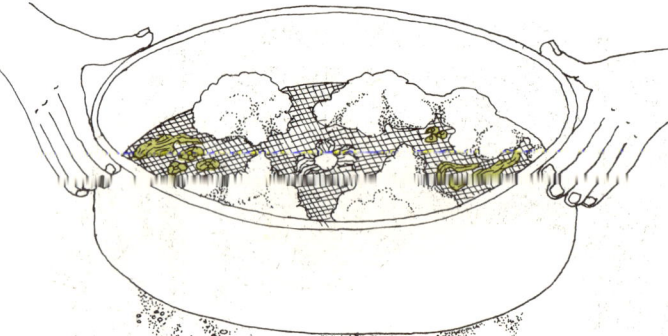

Dump the sand in your sieve. Swish it in the sea until the sand is rinsed out. See what sand creatures are left behind.

When you tip the creatures back on the sand they dig themselves out of sight in seconds.

Check that the shells you find are empty. If the hard cover over a shell's opening is tight shut leave the shell on the beach close to the water.

Some shore lines no longer have any shellfish because people have gathered them for too many years.

Beaches near cities are often so dirty that you will have to look hard for signs of life.

Even beaches far from people are in danger. Floating oil from ships kills sea life and smears the rocks and sand on the shore.

Sea birds' feathers can get so oily that the birds can hardly move. When they try to clean themselves they swallow the oil and are poisoned.

If you find a stranded bird, contact an animal welfare society at once. Saving the bird's life takes a lot of time and is very difficult. Only try this if you cannot get help from experts. Sometimes it is kinder to kill a badly oiled bird.

You will need to handle the bird very gently. It will already be shocked and afraid.

1 Wrap the bird in a soft towel leaving its head and feet free.

2 The bird may be starving. Feed it with cod liver oil and small strips of fish. Put the food well down inside the beak at the back of the throat.

3 Stand the bird in a bath of lukewarm water (40°C). Add ¼ cup of detergent to every bucket of water you use.

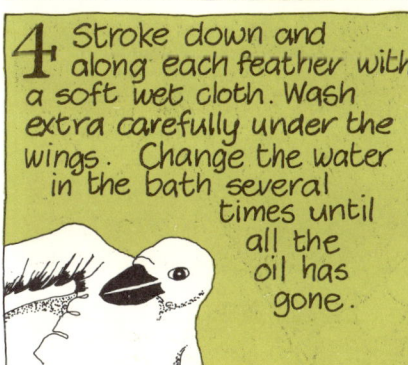

4 Stroke down and along each feather with a soft wet cloth. Wash extra carefully under the wings. Change the water in the bath several times until all the oil has gone.

5 Rinse the bird with more lukewarm water until every trace of detergent is removed. This may take as long as an hour. Dry carefully and rub hand lotion gently into legs and feet.

6 Keep the bird in a warm place until thoroughly dry. Then watch it outside for about 10 days. Give it plenty of food and water. Choose a fine day to set it free.

A patch of earth

The earth is full of life. No matter how bare it looks things are happening underground. Worms and insects are at work deep down. Seeds are waiting for the soil to feel just right for growth to start.

Clear a patch of earth for yourself and see what grows there. Choose a patch in a sunny place where people don't walk.

Pull out all the weeds and stones and twigs. Then turn the earth over with a spade.

Work the earth with your hands or a garden fork until it is fine and crumbly.

Build a low fence to mark your patch. If the weather is dry, water the ground often.

Now watch and wait. You may not see anything for several weeks. If it is very cold in your part of the world, spring will bring the first signs of life.

Seeds will begin to sprout and their shoots appear. There might be a bulb waiting deep underground. Seeds may blow in from weeds and trees nearby.

After a while it will be hard to see where your bare patch of earth has been. Now you can watch the strongest plants crowd out the weak ones.

and a jar of water

A jar of water will grow things if left to itself in a shady place.

Pond or even puddle water is full of life. Things you can't see are waiting their time to grow into water plants and creatures. Tiny eggs of frogs and fish and insects may be floating there, too.

Collect a jar of water from a weedy place and see what grows in it.

Even ordinary tap water will grow things if left to itself.

Tiny algae plants make green slime.

Cages

Never touch a house mouse. They spend time around garbage and will bite if afraid. See a doctor if you are bitten.

Mice know that people spell trouble. You have to work hard at teaching them that you are friendly.

You could keep a mouse in a cage like this for a few days while it gets to know you.

Cages worry wild creatures. No matter how safe and comfortable, life in a cage can never be the same as freedom.

But you can use cages carefully for a short time. This lets you have a close look at some of the creatures that live around you.

Anything you catch should be set free as soon as possible. Let terrified creatures go at once.

Make the cage as much like the creature's real world as you can. Check if it likes damp places or stones to shelter under. Try to watch it eating before you catch it so you can give it the things it likes best.

You can make friends with small wild animals if you have lots of time. Even in city places there are bound to be house mice around.

All mice were field mice once. Then, long ago, people began to stay in one place. They built shelters and harvested grain – and the mice stayed around. Now mice can be found almost anywhere there are people and food.

Good places to keep watch for mice are sheds where grain is stored. Warm places in houses attract them, too. Look underneath stoves or hot water services.

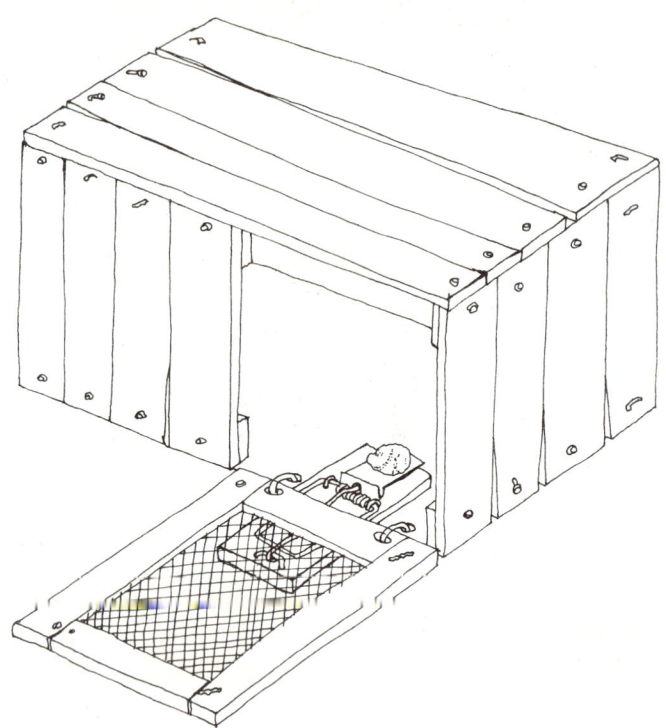

Make a small cage with a hinged door. Use a bird cage, or a large biscuit tin with a hinged lid. You could make your own hinges with a piece of wire.

Then you need a strong rat trap. Set the cage like this.

Insects can live quite happily for a while in an airy cage.

But don't keep them indoors for too long. They need the feel of fresh air to tell them whether the season is changing. It may be their time to lay eggs or to hibernate.

You will need some wire mesh and a straight-sided saucepan to make a cage.

Cake tins can make the top and bottom, too.

Make a tall funnel of wire to fit inside the saucepan. Lace the mesh together at the join with a strand of wire or string.

The saucepan lid goes on top of the wire.

A small jar of water can stand in the saucepan to hold a bunch of greenery. Collect some from where you found the insect.

There may be small lizards living near you. Look in piles of wood in sunny places.

A cardboard box with a lid can make a temporary lizard cage.

Never put lizards in a wire cage. They can injure themselves trying to escape.

Put a layer of gravel in the bottom of the box and sink a small dish of water into it. Some larger stones or pieces of wood make a hiding place. Cover the box with a piece of mosquito netting.

Cut a square hole in the lid and hold it on over the net with 2 rubber bands.

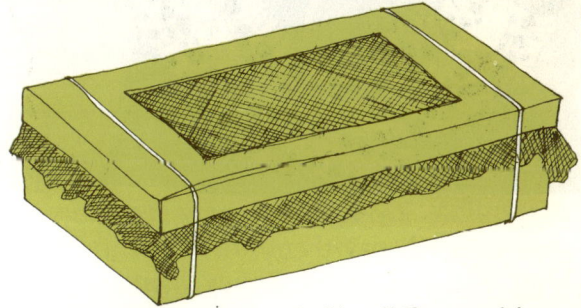

Different kinds of lizards like different things to eat. Let yours go after half a day – it gets hungry.

Handle lizards very carefully – their tails can fall off. They need to save this trick for real danger in the wild.

Caterpillars

For the first month after hatching, a caterpillar does nothing but eat and grow.

At the end of this hungry month, a caterpillar makes itself a hard case. Safe inside, next summer's moth or butterfly forms.

The best way to see all this happening is to make a watching net around a plant or a leafy branch. Choose one with lots of caterpillars and give them plenty of room.

Caterpillars are such everyday creatures that we don't pay them much attention – which is exactly what they want.

Caterpillars are designed to be left alone by birds and people. Some are hairy and hard to swallow. Some are fiercely striped and coloured. Some match the plants they live on. Some weave themselves hard cases from twigs.

A collecting box could be made for them instead. You will need a good supply of food caterpillars like. Collect some of the leaves you found them on. Give them fresh leaves whenever the old ones droop.

Leave space so the new moths or butterflies won't damage their wings when they first squeeze out of the caterpillar case.

Then let them go so they can lay eggs which will hatch out into more caterpillars.

Put a layer of clean sand or earth in the box.

Punch small holes in clear plastic food wrap. Hold it over the top of the box with elastic.

Aeolian harp

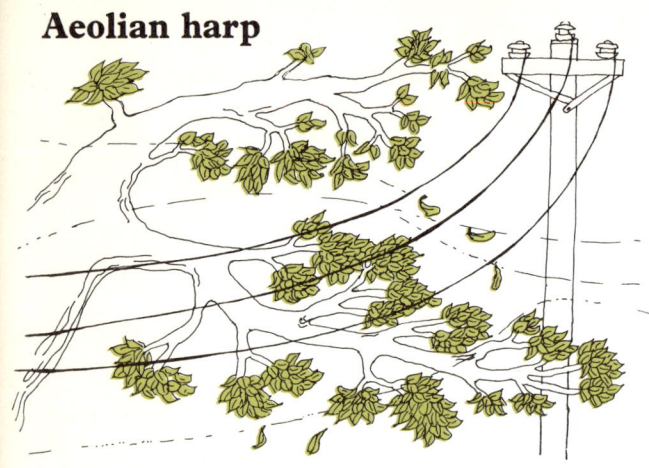

You will need
2 pieces of pine wood to fit your window
(about 140 mm wide and 18 mm thick)
2 pieces of the same wood about 40 mm long
2 pieces of wooden rod about 15 mm thick
12 large screw eyes, some thin 50 mm nails
1 set of guitar strings, a hammer, a drill and
a drill bit the same size as the screw eyes

People don't give the wind much thought most of the time. It has to be really whistling through the telephone wires or blowing us off balance to be noticed.

Here is a way to make an aeolian harp to remind you of the wind. This is an ancient instrument that plays music when the wind blows. Strange soft sounds can be heard as the strings vibrate.

People long ago thought there was something magical about the aeolian harp. Certainly the sound it makes seems to come from nowhere.

The best place for catching even the gentlest breeze is in the bottom of a partly open window. You could try the harp in a tree or on a wall outside, too. Choose a quiet place or the music could be drowned out.

If your harp is to go in a window, make it an exact fit. That way all the wind is funnelled through the harp. Measure the inside of the window frame.

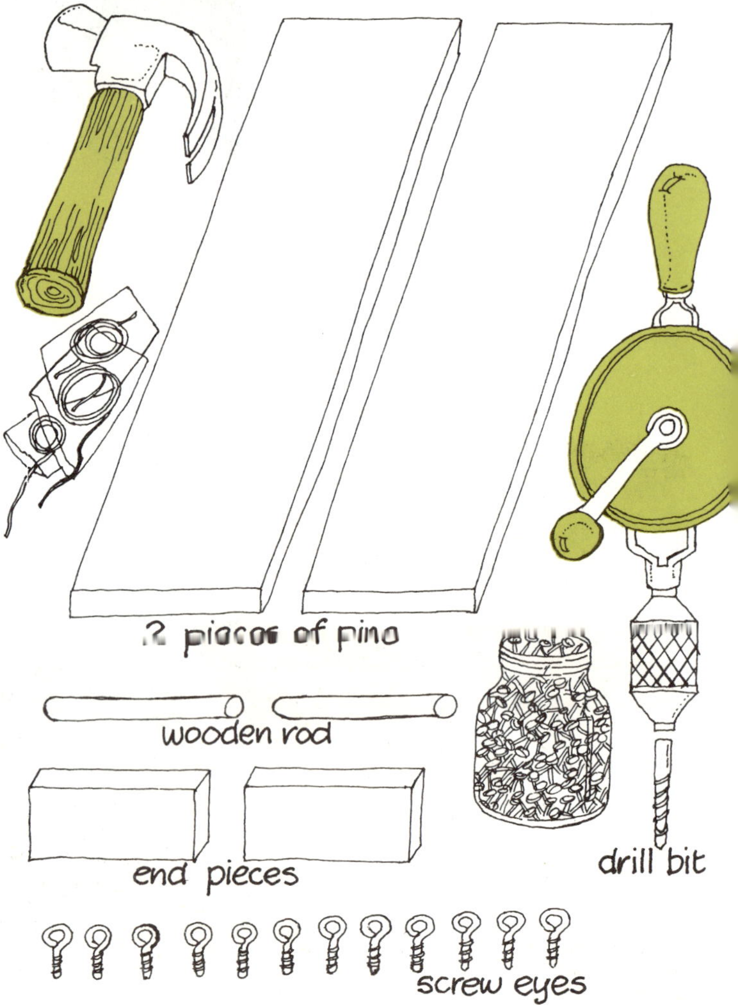

2 pieces of pine

wooden rod

end pieces

drill bit

screw eyes

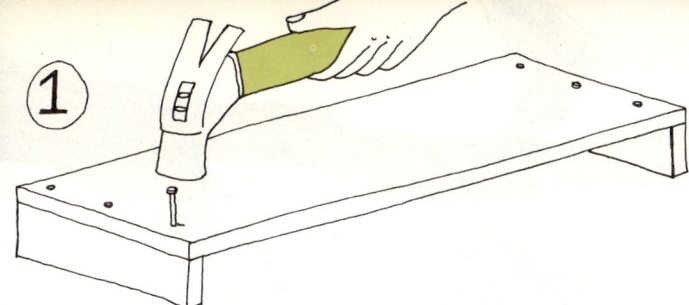

Nail the end pieces to one of the long boards.

Mark 2 lines about 5 cm from the ends and drill holes for the screw eyes.

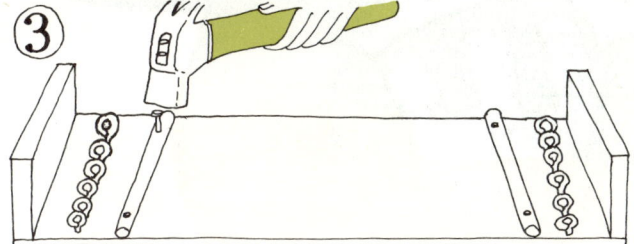

Screw in the screw eyes. Nail the wooden rods about 5 cm from them.

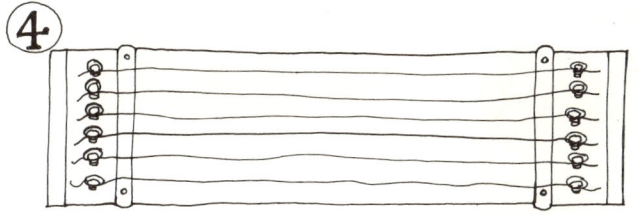

Tie the guitar strings to the screw eyes in order of thickness.

Fasten the top in place with one nail. It swivels so you can tune the strings easily.

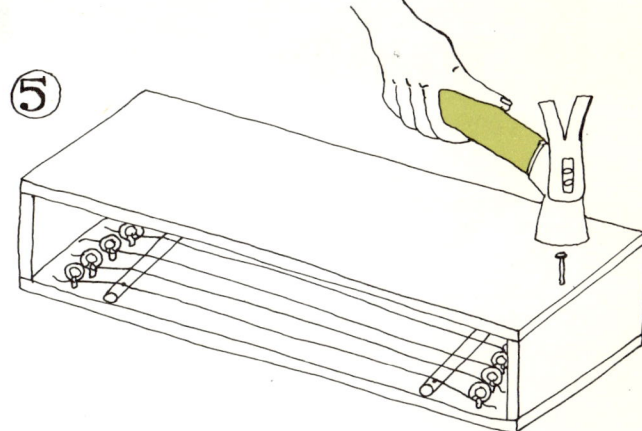

To tune your harp, start with the thinnest string. Turn the screw eyes until the string sounds a low note when you pluck it.

Then tighten the other strings until they make the same note. The thick strings will be tighter than the thin strings.

Put the aeolian harp at the bottom of an open window. Shut the window to hold the harp in place. Or fasten it firmly in a tree.

Wait for the wind to blow. At first you will hear a gentle hum. Listen as the wailing sounds start to build up as the strings vibrate. The sound will come and go with the wind.

Initialled fruit

Ripen your initials on the skin of an apple or a plum before it is picked.

Choose a piece of fruit that is still green and growing on a sunny branch.

Use coloured tape to shape your initial or make cut-outs from something that the sun can't shine through. Foil glued on works well.

If you have no fruit tree, buy a green tomato. Initial it and leave it on a sunny window sill.

Peel off the tape when the fruit is red.

Spider web

Here is a way to gather a web to keep.
Don't take one that a spider is still using.
Wait until you find an empty web. Early
morning is a good time to search.

Test some clear glue before you start. Glue
that is shiny when it dries is no use. The
web will vanish.

Have everything ready beforehand.
You will need
a smooth sheet of black cardboard
a piece of glass the same size
some clear glue
some tape for the edges

When you find your web, cover the card
with a thin coat of glue.

Cut the side threads with scissors to free
the web.

Place the card very gently behind the web
so it sticks to the gluey surface.

When the glue is dry you could cover the
card with glass and tape the edges.

A private place

Neighbourhoods are full of places that nobody uses much. Sometimes vacant land or old shops are left for years.

You and your friends might be able to build a private place.

Ask around to find out who owns the place you want to use. If you tell the owners what you want to do, they are less likely to make you move on later.

Ask at your local shop for the name of the owner, or go to your city centre. There will be records of names and addresses of owners in your area.

The more of you wanting to use the place the better. People don't take much notice of one or two kids.

Get help collecting building materials, too. People often have all kinds of junk they don't use.

Collect planks, crates, large drain pipes, strong cartons, sheets of roofing iron, old furniture, car tyres, nails, tools, rope, gardening things, and buckets.

Pull rusty nails out of wood before you use it. Keep stacks of things low so they won't fall over.

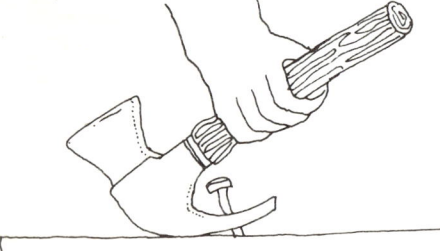

Make sure what you build is strong and safe. That way people won't panic about you.

Test everything with double the weight it's going to hold. Two people can jump on a plank on bricks or swing on a rope. If what you test creaks and cracks use something else.

Grow things, too. You might find part of an old garden choked with weeds, or cracks in walls and paths with strange plants in them. Encourage them by keeping the earth soft and watered.

A metal garbage bin lid makes a swing. Hang it close to the ground from a strong branch.

come in

go away

Birds

If there aren't many birds where you live, it is probably because the things they need have been bulldozed to make way for buildings. Most birds need nesting places, water holes, trees with seeds or nectar-filled flowers.

Some birds learn to live with the changes people make. They roost on the edges of high-rise buildings instead of cliffs or tree tops. Some build their nests in drain pipes instead of hollow branches. But most leave for the open spaces or stop breeding and die out all together.

You can slowly bring birds back to your area by giving them the things they need.

If you have a garden try planting things to attract birds. Choose the kinds of trees, bushes and grasses that have always grown in your part of the world. These are called native plants. They will attract native birds.

Put food out regularly and birds will soon get to know about it and come from miles around.

Bread, cheese, bacon rind, broken nuts and sultanas are things birds like. Leave out a small dish of water, too.

A hose dripping into a bowl on a hot day makes a bath for birds to splash in.

You can make a nectar mixture for honey-eaters. Mix four spoonfuls of clean water with every spoonful of honey.

Try building a nesting box. You might get birds to nest where you can watch them. Make your box in the autumn. Then a bird will have time to get to know it before nesting time in spring.

Some birds will nest in almost anything that gives them shelter – even an old boot or a saucepan in a bush.

For other birds the nesting box must be just the right size, or just the right height above the ground. Get advice from someone who knows the birds in your area.

Try a flower pot nesting place for small birds such as tits and sparrows.

Drill a hole about 3 cm wide in the middle of a square board. You can do this with a small drill bit. Draw a circle the size you want. Drill small holes close together around the edge. Knock the centre out and smooth the edge with a rasp or sandpaper.

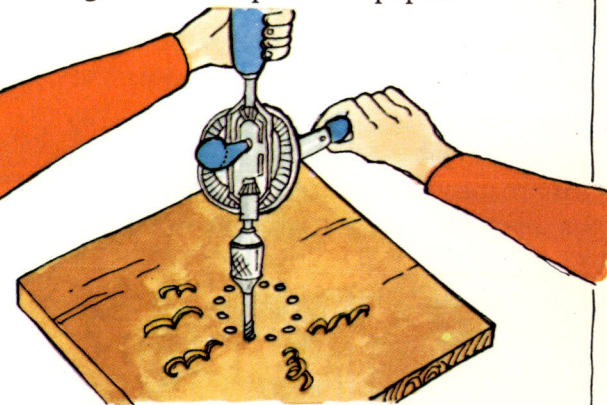

Wire the board over the top of a medium-sized flower pot.

Wedge the pot in a tree or creeper-covered fence.

Prospecting

The earth is rich in rocks of many different kinds and colours. The ones that are hardest to find are those that people want most.

Collect any kinds of rock you like. Some are shining and glass-like. Some have strange patterns and shapes and colours.

You can prospect for shining pebbles and fragments of special stones in rocky places.

Make yourself a collection of prospecting tools. You will need a flat dish or frying pan for prospecting in water, a sieve and some digging and picking tools.

panning dish

sieve

tweezers

garden trowel

prospector's pick — you could use a hammer

sticky tape

wire scraper — make one from a coat hanger

collecting jar

Shallow stream beds at the foot of hills or cliffs sometimes have stones washed down between the rocks.

Look where a stream flows over a rocky ridge, too. Small stones carried by the water catch on the ridge and fall to the bottom.

Scrape behind the rocky ridge with a garden trowel. Scratch in cracks between the rocks with a scraper.

Hunt in dry stony places with a trowel and a scraper, too. Large stones can be cracked open with a pick to see what's inside.

Tiny stones can be picked up with tweezers and carried home in a jar or inside a fold of sticky tape.

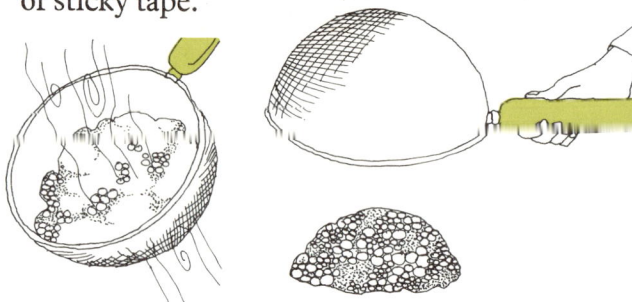

Any soil you collect can be sieved to make sure you haven't missed anything.

Wash the soil through a fine kitchen strainer in a stream – or under a tap at home.

Panning is the way much gold was found in stream beds long ago.

Stones that are heavier than sand can be sorted out in a panning dish.

HOW TO USE A PANNING DISH

1 Scrape down close to a layer of rock or clay. Half fill your pan with sand and gravel.

Break up lumps with your fingers.

2 Fill the pan with water and swirl it around. The heaviest pebbles will begin to fall to the bottom.

3 Pour off the water. Gently wipe away the top layer of sand and pebbles with the side of your hand.

4 Dip the pan into the water and swirl it. Wipe off another layer. Do this again and again until all the mud and clay is gone.

5 Hold the pan under flowing water. Swirl it around so the lightest gravel and sand is carried away.

6 Lift the pan out when just a handful of sand is left. Pour off all but a cupful of water.

7 Move the pan round and round. Tilt it from side to side, too.

The heavy stones will stay in the centre.

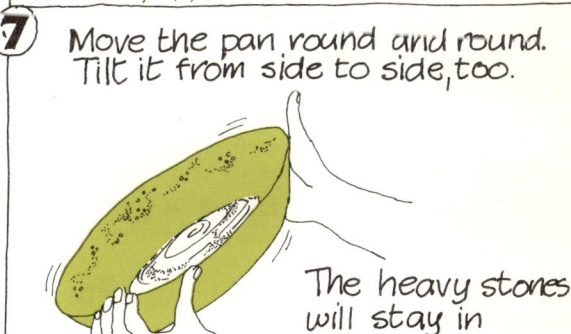

Neighbourhood games

These games or games like them have been played for hundreds of years by people in many countries. Anyone who knows some secret places in their neighbourhood can play.

The games can go on for hours and no one really wins in the end. You will need at least five people to start but dozens could play. In some places the whole village joins in.

Shine a light

This is a game for a dark night. Everyone gathers where the lights from houses and streets can't reach.

Two or three people are chosen as the torch bearers. They will need a flashlight or a hurricane lantern.

The torch bearers go off into the darkness with their lights turned off or hidden from sight. The hunters count to 50 slowly and the hunt is on.

When the hunters think they are close to the torch bearers they call out 'Shine a light'. The torch bearers flash a light then race off to a new hiding place.

The torch bearers keep the hunters on the run until they are caught or they get back safely to the start. You can set a time limit or play all night.

After a long hunt the torch bearers and the hunters can change over.

Tracking

This is a daylight game.

Gather at a starting place and divide into two gangs.

One gang goes off to be hunted. The others are the trackers. They count to 300 slowly to give the others a long start.

The gang being hunted leaves arrows for the trackers to follow. One person takes long strides and after every twenty strides makes an arrow.

The trackers rub out the arrows as they pass them.

Arrows can be chalked on fences, pavements and buildings or scratched with a stick in soft ground. Make arrows out of sticks, stones, anything lying around. Collect things as you run.

One of the hunted gang can leave the others and lay a false trail. This ends with a large cross to send the trackers back.

When the hunted gang comes to a place where they can all scatter and hide easily, they make one last sign – maybe four arrows in a bunch.

Then the trackers are on their own. They must find all of the other gang without any signs to help.

Dirty water

The world's water is getting dirtier and dirtier. Fish and birds and animals and people need water to survive.

You can find out how clean a freshwater creek or river is by looking at the small creatures that live there.

A few things can live in very dirty water. Others die if their water changes in any way.

You will need a small net. Make one from thin wire and a piece of nylon stocking.

Cut the stocking off above the knee and tie a tight knot in the narrow end.

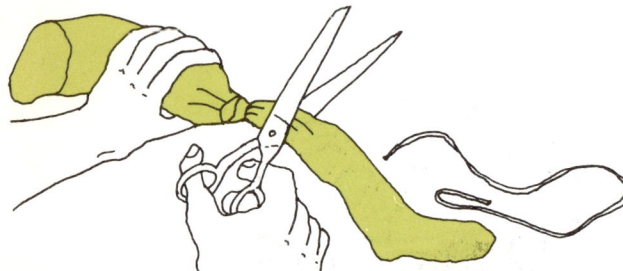

Thread the wire in and out around the top. The two ends of the wire are twisted around a long stick to make a handle.

Find a collecting dish with a white bottom. This shows up the tiny creatures you will find.

Choose a shallow place on the water's edge away from steep, slippery or crumbling banks.

Fill your dish with the clearest water you can see.

Now scoop your net through any weeds that are growing in the water. Lift stones and swish under them, too.

Clear as much mud from your net as you can with one sweep of water.

Now gently tip the things left in your net into your dish.

No creatures at all means badly polluted water. This water is poisonous.

Lots of different creatures means clean water.

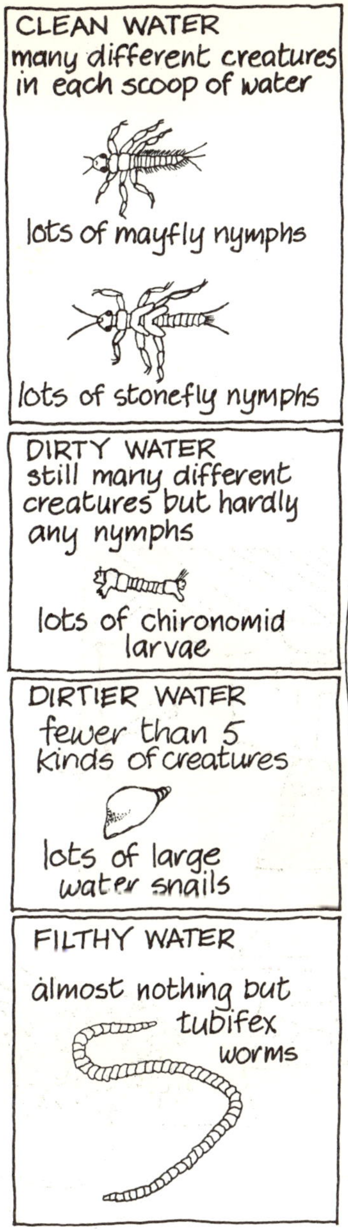

CLEAN WATER
many different creatures in each scoop of water

lots of mayfly nymphs

lots of stonefly nymphs

DIRTY WATER
still many different creatures but hardly any nymphs

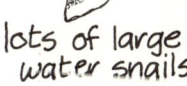

lots of chironomid larvae

DIRTIER WATER
fewer than 5 kinds of creatures

lots of large water snails

FILTHY WATER
almost nothing but tubifex worms

Test the water in three or four places along the bank to check your results. Downstream from a sewage pipe will be worse than upstream.

Dirty air

There have always been things floating in the air for us to breathe – pollen from plants, dust, sand, smoke from bushfires and fireplaces.

Our noses are lined with small damp hairs to trap these things and to keep them out of our lungs. But we can't filter out city air any more.

Have a close look at some of the things cars and trucks put into the air.

Make a filter for the exhaust pipe of a car or truck. A white sock or a handkerchief works best. Tie the filter over the exhaust pipe.

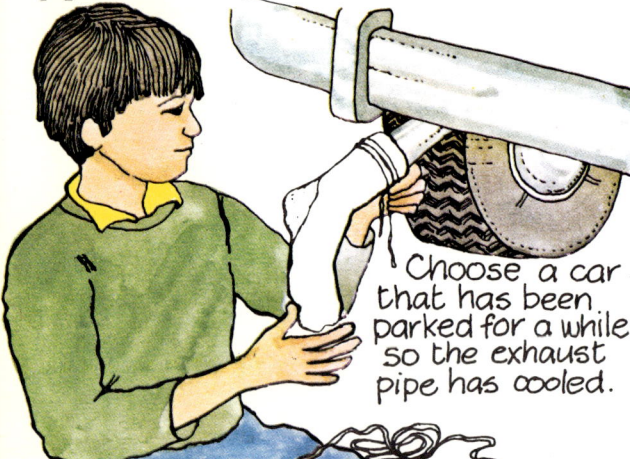

Choose a car that has been parked for a while so the exhaust pipe has cooled.

Ask the driver to turn on the engine for one minute.

When the engine stops take off the filter carefully – the exhaust pipe will be hot.

Look inside the filter. What you see is only part of what we breathe in – the rest is invisible.

One of the very worst air polluters is invisible. This is sulphur dioxide gas which kills plants, gives people bronchitis and eats away at buildings.

If you have two silver-plated spoons you can test for this gas.

Polish both the spoons until they are shiny clean.

Find a place to hang one spoon where there is heavy traffic. Keep the other spoon inside.

Compare the spoons after a week. If your area has sulphur dioxide gas in the air, the outside spoon will be grey and tarnished.

FRUIT

You can measure the amount of grit in the air in different places.

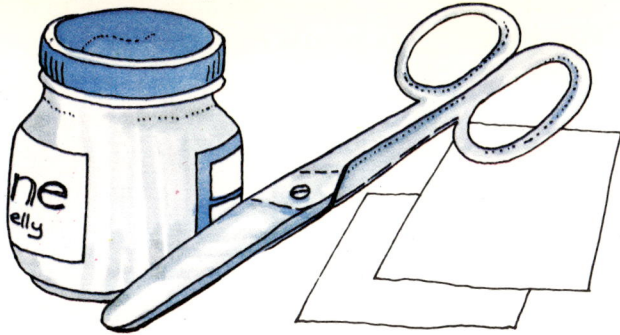

Cut a piece of white cardboard into squares. Cover one side of each square with a thin coating of Vaseline.

Pin up one square in your room. Others could go near a busy street corner, or maybe up a tree in a city park.

Hang a square on each side of the tree to see where the grit comes from.

If you know a smoking factory, nail a square nearby. The people in charge might take some notice if you can show them the grit they cause.

The grit sticks to the Vaseline. Check the cards at the same time next day to see which places have the dirtiest air.

Quiet times

Early morning or late at night are good times to inspect the living things around your place.

Many small creatures only come out at night. Be very quiet and you will see and hear a lot happening.

Make a screen for seeing insects clearly. You will need a flashlight, some blue cellophane and a white sheet.

Wrap the blue cellophane around the torch light and fasten it with a rubber band. Insects seem to like blue light best.

Hang the sheet over a branch or railing. Now prop the light on the ground so it shines on the sheet.

Insects will fly towards the blue light and crawl on the sheet. On warm nights you will see many different kinds of insects.

Use a flashlight to look for small animals, too. Shine it around you in a large circle and wait until you see eyes. The animal will probably be dazzled by the light. You will be able to creep up closer and watch it properly.

Watch the night sky, too. The stars, if you look hard enough, are different colours. The newest, hottest stars shine with a white light. Older, cooler stars have a reddish or yellow glow.

Find a high place to watch the sun come up. As the sky lightens you will see that red colours show up first in the things around you.

This is because you are seeing the light from a low angle across the earth. Blues are seen more clearly as the sun gets higher in the sky.

Dawn for many creatures is the time to disappear. Animals that hunt can be seen creeping back to their holes for the day.

Snails and slugs slide into a safe place at dawn to sleep off their night-long feast.

Many early morning signs of life disappear or get damaged later. Look for spiders' webs, dew on the grass, snail tracks and wet prints on concrete paths. Bird and animal footprints can sometimes be seen in muddy places near water.

People come out early in the morning, too. Papers and milk might be delivered early in your area – or streets swept clean or garbage taken away. Many people start work before it is light, or come home from working all night.

The best way of all to watch your neighbourhood at these times is to sleep outside.

Choose a warm night and a sheltered place in your yard or balcony. You will need a sleeping bag or a thick blanket. Even warm nights can get very cold after a while.

Food helps pass the time and keeps you warm. Potatoes hot from the oven are good things to have in your pockets.

Stay awake as long as you can. This is hard to do if you are waiting for something to happen. If your eyes keep shutting, try sitting in a really uncomfortable position.

Garden snails

Garden snails have a bad name. Their rasping tongues covered in tiny teeth grate big holes in people's gardens.

No two snails are exactly alike. Their shell patterns and colours are their own.

Snails come out at night. Dark leafy places and under flower pots and logs make daytime hide-outs.

You can have a snail race on your own or with friends. Look for the most wide-awake snails and mark a racing ring on a path.

The champion snail is the one that gets outside the racing ring first. This can take a long time. You may need cabbage or lettuce lures to get them moving.

Snails often go back to the same hide-out each day. Try to see where the champion goes so you can race it next time.